COUNTRY GARDENS
COLORING BOOK

TERESA GOODRIDGE

DOVER PUBLICATIONS, INC.
MINEOLA, NEW YORK

The countryside beckons in this lavishly illustrated coloring book, offering an array of lush gardens, overflowing flower pots and planters, comfortable outdoor seating, and even an appetizing table of mouthwatering delicacies. The inviting coloring pages offer a variety of beautiful blooms, as well as palm trees and various cacti. Dogs, cats, birds, bunnies, and butterflies feel right at home in these cozy surroundings—and so will you! The pages are printed on one side only and are perforated for easy removal.

Bibliographical Note

Country Gardens Coloring Book is a new work,
first published by Dover Publications, Inc., in 2020.

International Standard Book Number

ISBN-13: 978-0-486-84045-1
ISBN-10: 0-486-84045-X

Manufactured in the United States by LSC Communications
84045X03
www.doverpublications.com
4 6 8 10 9 7 5 3
2020